FIRE FROM HEAVEN

Terry W Sisney

Fire From Heaven

© 2017 by Terry Sisney. All rights reserved.

No part of this book may be reproduced in any written, electronic, recording, or photocopying without written permission of the publisher or author. The exception would be in the case of brief quotations embodied in the critical articles or reviews and pages where permission is specifically granted by the publisher or author.

Or through: createspace.com

Publication date: May 15, 2017

Language: English

Publisher: CreateSpace Independent Publishing Platform

ISBN: 9781546644989

From The Over Comers Series Vol 2

Table of Contents

Preface   04

1. Fire From Heaven ………………………………………….. 05

2. Keepers Of The Flame ……………………………………...15

3. Fight Fire With Fire ………………………………………25

4. Don't Waste Your Anointing ……………………………….34

5. Where There Is No Altar The Church Will Falter …………..70

6. Tarry Until ………………………………………………..84

About The Author

Other Books By The Author

Preface

I am writing this book because I am very concerned about the spiritual condition of the church today.

It is very difficult sometimes to come to grips with what our true condition is, but nothing will ever change until we are willing to be honest with ourselves.

In the natural, when we look in the mirror we are able to see our natural reflection. We are able to groom ourselves and take care of our natural appearance.

On the spiritual side, there is also a mirror. That mirror is the Word of God. When we look into the mirror of the Word of God we are not only able to see who we are, but also who we are supposed to be.

The Word of God shows us not only where we are missing it, but also how to get it right.

There is no doubt that the church today is a poor reflection of our birthright. In other words, the majority of the church world, as it exists today, is a very weak representation of the New Testament church.

There will never be any progress made toward our inheritance and our spiritual birthright until we look into the mirror of the Word of God and see what the church is supposed to look like. We must honestly assess ourselves according to the Word of God.

This book is just my small effort to help us, together, look honestly at ourselves, what we have, and who we are - in contrast to what God says we can have and can be.

Chapter One

Fire From Heaven

According to the Bible, our God is fire.
Our God is a consuming fire. (Hebrews 12:29).

It is not up for discussion. It is not negotiable. Organizations and denominations may defy it, deny it, neglect it and reject it. But they cannot change it.

All through the Bible, God reveals himself as fire.

God's presence among His people is always connected to fire.

He was the pillar of fire that went before the children of Israel on their wilderness journey.
And the LORD went before them by day in a pillar of a cloud, to lead them the way; and by night in a pillar of fire, to give them light; to go by day and night. (Exodus 13:21).

God spoke to them out of the fire.
And mount Sinai was altogether on a smoke, because the LORD descended upon it <u>in fire</u>: and the smoke thereof ascended as the smoke of a furnace, and the whole mount quaked greatly. (Exodus 19:18).

And the LORD spake unto you <u>out of the midst of the fire</u>: ye heard the voice of the words, but saw no similitude; only ye heard a voice. (Deuteronomy 4:12).

He was the fire that came down from heaven and consumed Solomon's offering.

Now when Solomon had made an end of praying, the fire came down from heaven, and consumed the burnt offering and the sacrifices; and the glory of the LORD filled the house.
(2 Chronicles 7:1).

In the New Testament, we find that the baptism of the Holy Ghost is a baptism with fire. (*Luke 3:16-17).*

As John was baptizing in the river Jordan he was heard to say: I indeed baptize you with water; but one mightier than I cometh, the latchet of whose shoes I am not worthy to unloose: He shall baptize you with the Holy Ghost and with fire:
  Whose fan is in His hand, and He will thoroughly purge His floor, and will gather the wheat into His garner; but the chaff He will burn with fire unquenchable.

When Jesus had ascended to the Father, and sent the mighty baptism of the Holy Ghost, He came as a rushing mighty wind and cloven tongues of fire.

And when the day of Pentecost was fully come, they were all with one accord in one place.
  And suddenly there came a sound from heaven as of a rushing mighty wind, and it filled all the house where they were sitting.
  And there appeared unto them cloven tongues like as of fire, and it sat upon each of them.
  And they were all filled with the Holy Ghost, and began to speak with other tongues, as the Spirit gave them utterance. (Acts 2:1-4).

He was the fire that fell on Mt. Carmel in answer to the prayer of Elijah.

Then the fire of the LORD fell, and consumed the burnt sacrifice, and the wood, and the stones, and the dust, and licked up the water that was in the trench. (1Kings 18:38).

Elijah, the prophet of God, comes on the scene of history when the children of God have fallen into gross sin.
Ahab, the King of Israel is a very wicked king. He leads the children of Israel into a lifestyle of idolatry. Then on top of all this, he marries Jezebel who is a witch, who introduces the children of Israel to Baal worship.

And Ahab the son of Omri did evil in the sight of the LORD above all that were before him.
31 And it came to pass, as if it had been a light thing for him to walk in the sins of Jeroboam the son of Nebat, that he took to wife Jezebel the daughter of Ethbaal king of the Zidonians, and went and served Baal, and worshipped him.
32 And he reared up an altar for Baal in the house of Baal, which he had built in Samaria.
33 And Ahab made a grove; and Ahab did more to provoke the LORD God of Israel to anger than all the kings of Israel that were before him. (1Kings 16:30-33).

The flame of God's presence among His people was at an all time low.

From the King, to the priests, to the prophets, there was corruption.
Israel, God's chosen people, had turned their backs on God.
The priests and the prophets were no longer the servants of God. They were serving their own selfish desires, their own lusts, and their own wills.
They were no longer attending to the altar of God.
The fire of God had all but gone out.

It was into this godless, lust driven, self serving, backslidden environment, that one lone prophet comes with a word from the Lord.

He calls for true repentance and pronounces a curse from God to fall upon the land until they repent.

And Elijah the Tishbite, who was of the inhabitants of Gilead, said unto Ahab, As the LORD God of Israel liveth, before whom I stand, there shall not be dew nor rain these years, but according to my word. (1 Kings 17:1).

The word of the Prophet is; until there is repentance, there will be no rain or even dew.

This natural drought was to reflect their spiritual condition.
Elijah emphasizes that it is their sins that have shut up the heavens over their land, and they will remain closed until there is national repentance.
Elijah then hides himself at the brook Cherith. He leaves Israel to wrestle with God.
To come to a decision; to humble themselves in true repentance and turn away from their sins. But Israel's heart is hardened. They have lost God consciousness. Their king is wicked. Their queen is a witch. Their prophets are false and their priesthood is profane.

But God, who is rich in mercy, is unwilling to give up on His people. So, He stirs the prophet Elijah again and sends him to King Ahab. He issues a challenge not only to Ahab, but to the whole rebellious nation and the perverse religious system that is in place, to meet him on Mt. Carmel.

At this point, Israel has been confronted with the Word of the Lord; they have suffered a prolonged drought and famine as a consequence of their sins.
But they are still undecided. There have been indications that they are now thinking about God, but they are vacillating back and forth between the altar of God and the altar of Baal.
They are indecisive, they are under strong delusion. Their prophets are under the control of Jezebel. The entire nation is under the influence of the spirit of witchcraft and religious manipulation.

Now the prophet of God, Elijah, the Man of God who stands before God and speaks for God, not only confronts Israel in their sins, but he stands alone on the mountain with God. He is in direct confrontation and opposition to the whole perverse and corrupt religious system, including king, queen, priests, and prophets.

Before Israel will turn back to God, this entire demonic, religious system must be exposed as false and counterfeit.
There is only one way.
There must be a witness from heaven. God Himself must testify. God Himself must answer the question and settle what is true and what is false.

There is only one way: Fire From Heaven.

The God of Israel - who is a consuming fire, who spoke to His people out of the fire, who supernaturally led His people in a pillar of fire, who fell from heaven and consumed Solomon's offering with fire, He must bring Israel to decision. There can be no gray area. God Himself will draw the line.

God Himself must make the decree. There must be a divine witness from heaven. Nothing less will melt the cold hearts of a backslidden nation.

All the preaching of the prophet, all the preparation that went before is insufficient to break the spell on their minds and turn them back to God.

As the prophet watches the false prophets go through all their rituals and ceremonies, he begins to taunt them, and agitate them.

And it came to pass at noon, that <u>Elijah mocked them</u>, and said, Cry aloud: for he is a god; either he is talking, or he is pursuing, or he is in a journey, or peradventure he sleepeth, and must be awaked. 28 And they cried aloud, and cut themselves after their manner with knives and lancets, till the blood gushed out upon them. (1Kings 18:27-28).

There is something powerful about knowing where you stand with God.

When you know where you stand with God, it troubles the enemy.

Finally, it's Elijah's turn and he prays a short prayer, and <u>the fire of God falls from heaven</u> and consumes the sacrifice, the wood, the altar, the stones, the water, and the dust.

The children of Israel fall on their faces crying, "The Lord He is the God, the Lord He is the God."

The prophet of God recognizes the tide has turned. God has turned the hearts of the people. He quickly urges them to destroy the false prophets.

With a fresh fire of holy zeal burning in their hearts, they join with the prophet of God and take all the false prophets down to the brook Kishon and kill them there.

<u>Then the fire of the LORD fell,</u> and consumed the burnt sacrifice, and the wood, and the stones, and the dust, and

licked up the water that was in the trench.
39 And when all the people saw it, they fell on their faces: and they said, The LORD, He is the God; the LORD, He is the God.
40 And Elijah said unto them, Take the prophets of Baal; let not one of them escape. And they took them: and Elijah brought them down to the brook Kishon, and slew them there. (1Kings 18:38-40).

The attitude in America today is much like it was in Israel at that time.
 There is such a perversity and profaneness that has entered the church.
The church today has become a hodgepodge of religious ceremonies and activities. There is much commotion, but there is little power; much noise, but little power; much to look at but little to see.
 The church, by and large, has settled for a form of godliness that denies the power thereof.
That means it looks good, it sounds good, it even feels good, but it is dead.
Once again the great need of the church is <u>fire on the altar</u>, not man's fire, but God's fire: fire from heaven.

It is no secret that man can produce a sort of a fire that can fool many people.
<u>But I will tell you who it cannot fool</u>:
It cannot fool the drug addict who is bound and can't make it through the day, without a drug being introduced into their bodies.
It cannot fool the homosexual and the lesbian who is crying out for deliverance.
It cannot fool the witches and the warlocks who are sick and tired of the devil destroying their lives.

It cannot fool the young man or young woman who is on the verge of committing suicide.
It cannot fool the prostitute who has been used and abused, and left alone in some hotel room, feeling worthless and forgotten.

    As a matter of fact, the only ones that are really being fooled are the religious ones that have lost the true <u>fire of Heaven</u> and have settled for a substitute. They have traded the power of God for the praise of men.
They're more concerned about being politically correct than Biblically correct. They're more concerned about fitting in than being right with God.
    What we need today is for the spirit of Elijah to rise up again, for men and women of God that will not compromise, that will not dilute God's Word, that will not back down to the spirit of religion, that will stand up and declare, "Thus sayeth the Lord."

What we need is for men and women, that have stood in the presence of God, to stand up and call God's people to decision.
It's time for decision. Who is on the Lord's side? Who is willing to be persecuted, lied on, rejected and despised for the sake of the Kingdom?

Is there anybody left who will stand up and say: Lord, send the fire?
Send the fire that will burn up sin. Send the fire that will burn hypocrisy out of the church.
Send the fire that will burn pornography out of our pulpits.
Send the fire that will burn adultery out of our pews.
Send the fire that will melt the hearts of the cold, dead, indifferent Christians that have settled for a shout with no clout.
They've settled for a form of godliness with no power.

Somewhere along the way, we have lost the definition of the church. The church is not just a charitable organization that is supposed to help feed the hungry, clothe the naked, and pay people's light bill.

All those things are good. (But the church was born in power.)
What kind of Power?
Fire from Heaven Power.
In that upper room in Jerusalem the church was born,
And the church was birthed in fire!
*Cloven tongues like as fire sat upon each of them. (Acts 2:3).
And they went out, and preached that men should repent. And they cast out many devils, and anointed with oil many that were sick, and healed them. (Mk 6:12-13).*

This is what Jesus said: The church in action looks like.
These signs shall follow them that believe, in my name shall they cast out devils, they shall speak with new tongues, and if ye drink any deadly thing it shall not hurt you, ye shall lay your hands on the sick and they shall recover. (Mark 16:17-18).

Jesus said: Ye shall receive power after that the Holy Ghost is come upon you, and ye shall be witnesses unto me both in Jerusalem and Judea and Samaria and unto the uttermost parts of the world. (Acts 1:8).

Jesus tells his disciples, *"Tarry ye in Jerusalem until ye be endued with power from on high." (Luke 24:49).*

If Elijah had not been supported with the fire of God from heaven, he would have died on that mountain.
The truth is: If we today are not supported with the fire of God from heaven, we are going to die.

We may have the most beautiful buildings and we may have the most gifted singers, and teachers and preachers, but if we don't have <u>fire from heaven</u>; we are already dead.

Chapter Two

Keepers Of The Flame

We all know that God is a consuming fire. We all know that we are to live a life on fire for God, but what we, at times, lose sight of is, God has made us responsible for our own flame.

And when the day of Pentecost was fully come, they were all with one accord in one place.
2 And suddenly there came a sound from heaven as of a rushing mighty wind, and it filled all the house where they were sitting.
3 And there appeared unto them cloven tongues like as of fire, and it sat upon each of them.
4 And they were all filled with the Holy Ghost, and began to speak with other tongues, as the Spirit gave them utterance.
(Acts 2:1-4).

One of the most exciting and powerful things that happened on the day of Pentecost was "every head got a flame."

I think one of our greatest failures as Christians is that so many fail to realize that God gives the flame, but it's our responsibility to keep, and tend the flame.

And the fire upon the altar shall be burning in it; it shall not be put out: and the priest shall burn wood on it every morning, and lay the burnt offering in order upon it; and he shall burn thereon the fat of the peace offerings. The fire shall ever be burning upon the altar; it shall never go out.
(Leviticus 6:12,13).

These verses tell us that it was the responsibility of the priests to keep the fire burning on the altar.

They were responsible to remove the ashes, the waste, the old, and the expired. Then, add new wood.

We are New Testament priests. We are now the keepers of the flame.

It is our responsibility to provide fuel for the fire. It is also our responsibility to get rid of the trash, to get rid of anything that threatens to quench or hinder the flame.

We have to see to it that every day we provide a fresh supply of wood.

The Holy Ghost comes to us as a flame that can either grow and develop, and become a devouring fire, or it can remain a small flicker. The Spirit can actually be quenched until He cannot be seen or experienced at all.

Just being in church doesn't stoke your fire, just hearing the preaching of the Gospel does not add any flame or fuel to your fire.

You can be in a place where miracles happen yet never receive a miracle. You can be where the presence of God is, and the power of God is moving, yet not be moved.

I recall a time when my wife and I, along with some other friends from the church, went to a brother and sister's house for fellowship after church. After we ate, we went outside to sing around the fire.

But there wasn't any fire, just a fire pit, and a pile of wood. No matter how long we looked at it and thought about it and wished we had a fire, nothing happened; nobody got warm, no marshmallows got roasted, until a lighter was put to the wood, and even that wasn't enough. They had to get some kindling and pour starter fluid all over the wood.

The same is true for you and me. We have to feed the fire. We have to add kindling and pour starter fluid all over it. That is something you have to do for yourself.

You say, how do I do that?

1. You have to have the Word, that's the kindling.

2. You have to pray, Pray until the fire falls, and then keep on praying until the flame begins to consume everything in your life.

Read the Word, study the Word, pray, praise, and worship.

Pray in tongues, sing in tongues, and worship in tongues.

Jude, verse 20, says: *But ye beloved building up yourselves on your most holy faith, praying in the Holy Ghost.*

You build up your inner being by praying in the Holy Ghost. You enlarge yourself, and you enlarge your capacity to receive.

You have to give yourself to the flame.

I beseech you therefore, brethren, by the mercies of God, that ye <u>present your bodies a living sacrifice, holy, acceptable unto God which is your reasonable service.</u> And be not conformed to this world: but be ye transformed by the renewing of your mind, that ye may prove what is that good, and acceptable and perfect, will of God. (Romans 12 1-2).

The Bible tell us of a man named Joash. He was a very important man.

And over the olive trees and the sycomore trees that were in the low plains was Baalhanan the Gederite: and <u>over the cellars of oil was Joash</u>. (1 Chronicles 27:28.)

He was important because he was the keeper of the King's oil.

Whenever the King, or the King's household, needed oil they came to Joash, he was in charge of the oil. Oil was used for almost everything. It was necessary for cooking, oil was also necessary for the lamps, to keep the lamps burning.

Well, that's what we are: Just like Joash, we are keepers of the King's oil.

Oil makes the fire burn. The oil is the fuel of the fire.

Being a keeper of the oil means,

<u>**We are responsible:**</u>

1. To be sure that there is always oil available.

2. To be sure that the oil is always fresh.

3. To keep the oil free of contaminants.

The Bible says: *dead flies cause the ointment of the apothecary to send forth a stinking savor. (Ecclesiastes 10:1).*

In other words: dead things, carnal things, selfish things, fleshly things make the anointing stink.

It doesn't matter how anointed you are, if you have carnality, fleshly things, earthly things (criticism, jealousy, envy, strife, debate, rebellion, anger, selfishness, stubbornness, resentment) it causes the anointing to stink.

<u>**In other words:**</u> your fleshly character can make your anointing, in-valid, or undesirable, this puts a bad reflection on Christianity itself.

The Christian is supposed to produce a sweet aroma, the Spirit of Christ is sweet, and pure, and honest, and precious; and draws people to Christ.

But a carnal, selfish, self-willed, critical, stubborn, argumentative Christian drives people away.

Many years ago kerosene lamps had to be tended to. First of all, they had to have kerosene. Then, they had to have the globe cleaned from time to time. Otherwise, when the wick got burned, instead of a beautiful clear light, it would smoke up the globe. And finally, they had to have the wicks trimmed ever so often.

The same is true for us; we have to make sure we have oil in our lamps.

We have to keep the wick trimmed, we have to cut off and cut out the unnecessary, the unprofitable, the used, the old, and the excess. And we have to keep the globe clean so people can clearly see the light in us, and not our fleshly nature.

Paul said (and I'm paraphrasing) there are a lot of things I could do and probably even get by with it because it's not necessarily sin, but I have decided to do only that which is profitable to my spiritual life, to do only that which serves to build and strengthen my faith and my relationship with God.

By the Spirit of God, Solomon said:

Let thy garments always be white and let thy head lack no ointment or anointing. (Ecclesiastes 9:8).

Let thy garments always be white.

The garments speak of the life that you live, that others can see, the outward expression of the inward possession.

If you claim to have the Holy Spirit living in you, then your life should show it.

David said: *Thou anointest my head with oil. (Psalm 23:5).*

Solomon said that your head should never be without the anointing. That means God is the one who anoints, but it is our responsibility to get in position for that anointing and to maintain it.

How do we maintain the anointing?

We accomplish this by:

- Spending time in His presence.
- Getting into His Word.
- Being in submission to His will.
- Praying in the Holy Ghost.

Not every head gets anointed,

God does not anoint: The stubborn head,

The self-willed head,

The rebellious head,

The religious head,

The lazy head.

He doesn't anoint the out-of- position head.

One of the most important ways to keep the anointing in your life is to be in position in the body of Christ.

All of our anointing comes from Christ, the anointed one, who is the head of the Church. He is the head of the entire body of Christ.

Christ means: the anointed one.

Then the anointing flows down to the local body <u>from the head</u> of the local body or assembly.

The pastor is the head of the local assembly.

The anointing flows down from the head (the pastor) to the rest of the body. That is why it's so important to be in the body and to be positioned under the right head.

When you speak of the head, you are speaking of vision, you are speaking of hearing, and you are speaking of voice.

In other words, God has made the pastor (the head) responsible for seeing God's plan and hearing God's instructions, and speaking His wisdom, and His direction, and His guidance for the local church.

That's why you shouldn't even listen to headless prophets

Headless prophets are lone rangers, people who believe they are so spiritual and so anointed, and so advanced that they don't need a pastor. They don't think they need a head.

Dear Friend:

I don't care if you are an apostle, prophet, pastor, teacher, evangelist, missionary or janitor. You are part of the body of Christ and you need to be under a pastor, an overseer, a shepherd. You need to be covered. That's what the head is; the head is a covering to you.

That's why it matters where you go to church and who you sit under.

Because if the head is not anointed, the body is not anointed. That is why you don't want a dead head.

If the head is dead, the whole body is dead.

I would rather sit under a self-taught farm boy who has the anointing, than a seminary professor with more degrees than a thermometer, but has no anointing.

Because Jesus said: *it is the spirit that quickeneth; the flesh profits nothing. (John 6:63).*

And the apostle Paul said: *The letter killeth but the spirit maketh alive. (2 Corinthians 3:6).*

It's not the degrees or education that makes alive, it is the anointing.

It's the anointing that destroys the yoke, not physiology or psychology, or even theology, it's the anointing! Specifically, it comes through the lifestyle of "kneeology."

I'm not putting down education or higher learning; I'm just saying that education is no substitute for the anointing.

Smith Wigglesworth said: if you're not moving forward, you're backsliding.

You're backsliding if you have to look back at your life to see a time when you were closer to God and more on fire for God, than you are today.

The Bible says: *the path of the just is as the shining light that shineth more and more unto the perfect day. (Proverbs 4:18)*

That means our light, our fire, is supposed to get bigger and brighter all the time until we are completely consumed, completely on fire for God.

- We were created for the fire.
- We were created to live in the fire.
- We were created to be creatures of fire.
- We were created to carry the fire.

It is the plan of God and the will of God that everything we touch catches on fire.

Remember the Flame?

His name was Johnny. He was one character of the Fantastic Four, a cartoon show we used to watch. He would say: flame on and he would burst into flames!!! He could fly while he was on fire, and he could throw fire, and everything he touched would catch on fire.

We are inclined to say: well that was a silly cartoon. And I would agree with you, that was just a cartoon.
But now, let's look at a Word from God.
It is not a cartoon.

We will find it in Ezekiel 1, verses 13-14.

This man of God, this prophet, this man who had his spiritual eyes open, had a vision.

Really, it was more of a revelation.

It was an unveiling of a Spiritual reality that God was bringing into being.

Actually, it was a prophetic vision of the New Testament Church filled with the Holy Ghost and power.

In this vision, in this revelation, he saw creatures of fire. He didn't really understand what he was seeing but he just described it as he saw it in the spirit.

First, he saw a great whirlwind of fire enfolding itself. It was a perpetual self-feeding fire. Next, he saw creatures moving around inside of the fire. Then he saw what looked like streaks of lightning that would shoot out from the fire and then return to the fire.

As he continued to see in this vision, he recognized that what looked like streaks of lightning were actually the same living creatures that were moving around inside the fire.

As for the likeness of the living creatures, their appearance was like burning coals of fire, and like the appearance of lamps: it went up and down among the living creatures; and the fire was bright, and out of the fire went forth lightning. And the living creatures ran and returned as the appearance of a flash of lightning. (Ezekiel 1:13-14).

These scriptures are a revelation of the church when she is walking in her destiny, anointed by fire.

Just like those living creatures, we were created to live in the fire. <u>The fire of God is our natural environment</u>. Just like those living creatures, we are to carry the fire of God everywhere we go.

Lightning speaks of two things: 1. Speed   2. Fire.

That is an accurate description of the Holy Ghost filled, fire baptized, Spirit led child of God.

We are to move like lightning, with speed and accuracy. We are to be on fire everywhere we go.

Because we are Keepers of the Flame.

Chapter 3

Fight Fire With Fire

Hell's fire is being unleashed on this earth like never before. How will the church respond? The answer is with fire.

So Moses and Aaron went to Pharaoh and did what the Lord had commanded them. Aaron threw down his staff before Pharaoh and his officials, and it became a serpent! 11 Then Pharaoh called in his own wise men and sorcerers, and these Egyptian magicians did the same thing with their magic. 12 They threw down their staffs, which also became serpents! But then Aaron's staff swallowed up their staffs. (Exodus 7:10-12).

There is a word jumping in my Spirit today.
It's just one word: FIRE!

If someone were to run into your house right now and yell, "FIRE," the whole atmosphere would change. Your heart would race. Your eyes would open wide. You wouldn't just sit there watching TV or eating dinner. You would be looking to see where the fire is, and where is the fire extinguisher?

I know that's a little graphic. But it's a fact and every bit of that activity would be natural and understandable, because your life could be in danger.

I want to speak to you now about a fire that we don't want to run from. We are not looking for a fire extinguisher and we're not looking for the exit signs.

I'm talking about a fire we need to be crying out for. I'm talking about the Fire of God, the Fire of the Holy Ghost.

John said: *The one who is coming after me is mightier than I and when He is come, He will baptize you with the HOLY GHOST and FIRE. (Matthew 3:11).*

What we're seeing in this text is a power confrontation: The power of Hell versus the power of God. (Or Hell versus Heaven! Or the fire of Hell versus Heaven's fire!)

I am compelled to tell you today: The church of the Lord Jesus Christ must catch on FIRE.

There is an unholy, satanic, demonic fire that is being unleashed in the earth today. And the sleepy, sloppy, passive, halfhearted, slumbering half-baked church and church members aren't qualified to deal with it.

It's going to take a Holy Ghost fire-baptized church that can pray Heaven down and cast Hell out.

Hell is on fire. The devil is sending his fire out against the church. In other words, the snakes are coming out of the woodpile. They're coming out of hiding. In other words, Hell's fire is loose.

And I'm telling you, that a bunch of wet blankets won't put it out.

You've heard the old saying: You've got to fight fire with fire. Well, it's true. There's nothing less than the fire of God that can put out Hell's fire.

Even Shakespeare spoke of this fire against fire.

He said: Be stirring as the time; be fire with fire; Threaten the threatener and outface the brow of bragging horror.

You may be thinking, Pastor Terry, you're laying it on pretty thick aren't you? Surely, it's not that bad.

Friend: If you believe that, you must be related to Rip Van Winkle, who fell asleep and woke up 20 years later and thought everything was the same as when he fell asleep.

Yes, it is that bad, and any pastor, any leader, any shepherd who does not sound the fire alarm to his or her sheep (and to anyone who will listen,) is failing in their call and is inviting disaster.

When witches are banding together and calling for the country to join them in casting spells, hexes, and curses against the president and the Supreme Court - we have a problem. And it's not just a disagreement of political parties. It's spiritual warfare.

The snakes are coming out of the wood piles!

The most important thing the ministry can do today is to equip the saints to fight. I believe in prosperity, but money is not the most important thing right now.

Like never before, it's time to pray and it's time to pray like never before.

Now I lay me down to sleep prayers won't work here.

If the church would have prayed those kind of wimpy, sleepy prayers for Peter, he would have died. But the church went into deep, spiritual warfare. They went into Heaven-shaking, Hell-breaking, unceasing prayer and God sent an angel who delivered Peter from the same fate that James suffered.

James was killed by Herod because the church was asleep.

It's time for the church to wake up. This is no time for the church to rest on her laurels. This is the time for the church to catch on fire.

I don't speak about the Holy Ghost and fire, just because I think it would be neat for you to speak in tongues. I speak about being baptized with the Holy Ghost and fire because Hell is being unleashed against the church and the world. The only thing that can qualify you, and equip you, and empower you, is the power of the Holy Ghost and fire.

Our God is a consuming fire.

He shall baptize you with the Holy Ghost, and with fire.

Who does He baptize with the Holy Ghost and fire? "Those who have been baptized in his blood".

The Holy Ghost baptism is a fire baptism.

You cannot separate the fire from the Holy Ghost.

Fire has always been a symbol of the Lord's presence among His people.

- God led the children of Israel through the wilderness, by a cloud by day and a pillar of fire by night.

- God appeared to Moses in a flame of fire out of the midst of a bush. (Exodus 3:2).

In Exodus 19:18, when God came down to speak to His people, the Bible says: And mount Sinai was altogether on a smoke, because the LORD descended upon it in fire: and the smoke thereof ascended as the smoke of a furnace, and the whole mount quaked greatly.

And the sight of the Glory of the Lord was like devouring fire on the top of mount Sinai in the sight of the people. (Exodus 24:17).

When Ezekiel saw the glory of the Lord, here is how he described it.

And upon the likeness of the throne was the likeness as the appearance of a man above upon it. 27 And I saw as the colour of amber, as the appearance of fire round about within it, from the appearance of his loins even upward, and from the appearance of his loins even downward, I saw as it were the appearance of fire, and it had brightness round about.

(Ezekiel 1:26, 27).

When Elijah left the earth, it was in a chariot of fire and horses of fire.

Fire has always been an identifying characteristic of the people of God.

And the fire upon the altar shall be burning in it; it shall not be put out: and the priest shall burn wood on it every morning, and lay the burnt offering in order upon it; and he shall burn thereon the fat of the peace offerings. (Leviticus 6:12).

The fire shall ever be burning upon the altar; it shall never go out. (Leviticus 6:13).

- Fire is Heaven's witness that we are God's property.

- Fire is Heaven's witness that God is in our midst.

- Fire is a purifier, fire illuminates, fire brings hidden things to light, fire empowers.

We talked about this earlier:

As Elijah met the false prophets of Baal upon Mt. Carmel, there was a great confrontation between religion and relationship, between a form of godliness and the power of godliness, between the works of men and the power of God.

Such was the confrontation, that there could only be one deciding factor. Who would answer by fire; let him be God. When Elijah had finished rebuilding the altar, preparing the sacrifice, setting the wood in order, and pouring water over the offering, he knew that he had done all he could on earth. He knew that it was still insufficient, and weak, and powerless to change the hearts of the people. If Heaven didn't bear witness, and testify with fire, he would probably be killed. Israel would be more vile than ever.

He prayed **and the fire fell.**

Fire is Heaven's answer to our prayers.

The Fire is Heaven's solution for our weakness.

Hear me, O LORD, hear me, that this people may know that thou art the LORD God, and that thou hast turned their heart back again. (1 Kings 18:37).

Fire is Heaven's witness to an acceptable sacrifice.

Any time God finds an acceptable sacrifice, He testifies and responds to it, and answers from Heaven by fire.

And David built there an altar unto the LORD, and offered burnt offerings and peace offerings, and called upon the LORD; and He answered him <u>from heaven by fire</u> upon the altar of burnt offering. (1 Chronicles 21:26).

Now when Solomon had made an end of praying, <u>the fire came down from heaven</u>, and consumed the burnt offering and the sacrifices; and the glory of the LORD filled the house. (2 Chronicles 7:1).

I beseech you therefore, brethren, by the mercies of God, that ye present your bodies a living sacrifice, holy, acceptable unto God, which is your reasonable service. (Romans 12:1).

Fire is contagious. As long as there is material, the fire will burn.

Where no wood is, there the fire goeth out: (Proverbs 26:20).

Wherever there are hungry hearts the fire will burn.

The fire of God will burn out of you everything that is not like God. The fire of God will burn out drug addiction, and anger, and lust, and fear, and unforgiveness, hate and prejudice, and pride.

There are too many people who want to know God just as a blesser. But God is not just a blesser.

<u>He is a possessor</u>. God wants to possess you. He wants to fill you and flow through you. He wants to make you a channel of His power.

For our God is a consuming fire. (Hebrews 12:29).

God wants to consume you. He wants to set you on fire, and make you a firebrand.

And of the angels He saith, Who maketh His angels spirits, and <u>His ministers a flame of fire. (Hebrews 1:7).</u>

And Samson went and caught three hundred foxes, and took firebrands, and turned tail to tail, and put <u>a firebrand</u> in the midst between two tails. 5 And when he had set the brands on fire, he let them go into the standing corn of the Philistines, and burnt up both the shocks, and also the standing corn, with the vineyards and olives. (Judges 15:4-5).

The definition of a <u>firebrand</u> is:

1. A piece of wood or material that is burning hot because it has just been taken out of the fire.

2. It is a piece of material that is carrying some of the fire that it has been in.

3. A firebrand is a person who causes unrest or is very energetic. In other words: A firebrand is a person, who is on fire and can stir others, can ignite others.

When the Holy Ghost came on the day of Pentecost, He came as a rushing, mighty wind and Tongues of Fire.

Why? Because God knew the church without power was no match for the devil. He knew that Hell's fire was burning against the church, and the only thing that could put it out was Fire from Heaven.

It is still true today, I pray about many things through the week, but at the top of my list and first in priority is; God send the fire, baptize me with fresh Holy Ghost fire, and baptize your church with the Holy Ghost and fire.

The fire of God is not a mental concept or idea to be analyzed by the mind.

The fire of God is the tangible manifested power of God invading the earth realm, consuming your mind, your soul, your body, and setting you on fire for His kingdom sake.

This is not a time for the Church to go AWOL. This is the time for the church to catch fire, and fight fire with fire.

You need to be so on fire today that anybody who gets near you can feel the heat. Especially the devil should feel the heat.

Let me ask you this question: Does Hell feel the heat coming from your prayer closet? Does Hell feel the flames of your prayers?

John Knox was a Scottish clergyman who shook Scotland with his prayers. His heart's cry was, give me Scotland else I die.

Mary the Queen of Scots said: I fear the prayers of John Knox more than all the assembled armies of Europe.

That is the kind of fire we need in the church again.

Let me ask you another question, dear friend. When are you going to get sick and tired of watching the devil run ram shod over this nation and over your children; stealing the innocence of little kindergarteners; murdering the unborn by the millions; twisting minds until they don't even believe they have the right body parts; believing that God put them in the wrong bodies, and worshipping Satan?

There is only one hope for this nation and it's not a Black hope and it's not a White hope. It's not the man sitting in the Oval Office. It is the man sitting on the throne of Heaven, the Man Christ Jesus; the King of kings and the Lord of lords.

He has invested the church with His power, He has made us responsible for bringing His will to the earth.

He said the church must pray for His Kingdom to come and His will to be done on the earth as it is in Heaven.

He said the church must bind and loose.

He said the church must cast out devils.

He said the church must heal the sick in His name.

He said the church must do the asking and He will send the fire.

Right there, where you are, my friend, just lift your hands and your voices right now and Put a demand on Heaven.
Tell God you know you need the fire.

Tell God you are desperate for the fire.

Tell God you're sick and tired of being sick and tired;

Sick and tired of the devil stealing and killing and destroying everything good.

Tell God you are ready to fight fire with fire.

Chapter Four

Don't Waste Your Anointing

As a minister of the gospel, and especially as a pastor, one of the saddest things, is to see someone that you know, without a shadow of a doubt, has the anointing of God upon their lives; yet, you see them waste their lives and waste the anointing in the pursuit of earthly fleshly pleasures.

Right now there are young men playing in night clubs, strung out on dope, who have the call of God upon their lives. There are young men in the crack houses, that <u>could</u> out preach a lot of preachers in the church. But they are running from God.

There are young ladies in houses of prostitution that are selling their bodies, who should be standing on platforms in our churches leading the saints of God in high praises. But they are yielding themselves to the devil.
Called of God but drunk, the hand of the Lord is over their lives, but they're hooked on crack; caught up in a world of lust and deception.

    I know that religious people have a problem with this; we think the only people God anoints are those who have got it all together, who are all dressed up and smelling good, and carry a twenty pound Bible under their arm. But I just have to take a minute and tell you that God doesn't just anoint perfect people.

David wasn't perfect, but he was anointed. He committed adultery with Bathsheba, but he was still anointed.
He had Bathsheba's husband killed, but he was still anointed.
    King Saul on several occasions tried to kill David, but Saul

was still anointed. Samson was anointed. He was always in the wrong place at the wrong time looking the wrong way. But he was anointed.

In no way, am I justifying a sinful life or a sloppy lifestyle. I'm just saying, God does not just anoint perfect people.

I am writing this book because I want to see the people of God live the anointed life. I want to help you walk in the full measure of the anointing of God for your life and not waste one drop of it.

As a born again, Spirit-filled, child of God, you should be experiencing the highest quality of life on the planet. No one should be happier, or more thankful, or more compassionate and considerate. No one should have more joy or more peace than you.

You are entitled to the highest quantity and the highest quality of life there is; not because of who you are but because of whose you are.

Jesus said: *I am come that they might have life and that they might have it more abundantly. (John 10:10).*

Strong's Exhaustive Concordance defines "abundantly" as: over and above, more than is necessary, superadded, supremely, something further, superior, extraordinary, surpassing, uncommon, pre-eminence, superiority, advantage, more eminent, more remarkable, more excellent.

This superadded, surpassing, extraordinary, more excellent life is found only one place. It is in the Holy Ghost.

The Holy Spirit is that source of life.

The overflowing, super abundant, extraordinary, more excellent life that every believer desires is in the anointing.

The anointing is the source of the abundant life.
David said: *Thou anointest my head with oil, <u>my cup runneth over.</u> (Psalm 23:5).*

The anointing was the source of power in Jesus' life.
How God anointed Jesus of Nazareth with <u>the Holy Ghost and with power</u>, who went about doing good and healing all that were oppressed of the devil for God was with Him. (Acts 10:38).

The anointing is the source of power in the believer's life.
But ye shall receive power after that the Holy Ghost is come upon you and ye shall be witnesses unto me... (Acts 1:8).

What is the anointing?
It is the supernatural endowment, enablement, and equipment of God, which He gives to a person, by the Holy Spirit, to accomplish His purpose. It may be to do something, to say something, to preach, to heal, to sing, to play an instrument, to do wonders, or miracles, to skillfully craft or build something, etc. The anointing affects every part of our being; the anointing touches our mind, our emotions, our talents, and our spirits.

All through the Old Testament there were occasions when the Spirit of the Lord, or the anointing, would come upon individuals, but it was only for a specific purpose for a limited period of time. Some examples are Samson, Gideon, and Elijah.

According to Strong's definition: "anoint" means to smear, to rub with oil, to consecrate, to paint, through the idea of contact.

Christ was not Jesus' last name. The word Christ comes from the word <u>christened</u> and it means, to anoint. Christ is the

Anointed One from which every believer derives their anointing.

Isaiah the prophet was speaking of Jesus when he said:
The Spirit of the Lord GOD is upon me; because the LORD hath anointed me to preach good tidings unto the meek; He hath sent me to bind up the brokenhearted, to proclaim liberty to the captives, and the opening of the prison to them that are bound. (Isaiah 61:1)
It is through contact with the living Christ that we become rubbed with the anointing.
As we spend time in the presence of Jesus, His anointing begins to soak into our lives, and we carry the anointing of His presence with us wherever we go.

Again Strong's defines the anointing as grease, especially liquid as from the olive. The olive is a symbol of prosperity.
(a) The anointing speaks of fatness, fruitfulness, richness, and fullness.
(b) It means to shine.
(c) It speaks of a special endowment.

Olive oil was the main ingredient for the lamps, used in Bible days. It was the olive oil that made the lamps shine.

One of best definitions of the anointing is, it furnishes what is needed.

Everything we need is in the anointing.
According as His divine power hath given unto us all things that pertain unto life and godliness. (2 Peter 1:3).
His divine power is the anointing of the Holy Ghost.
The bible says:
How God anointed Jesus of Nazareth with the Holy Ghost and

with power: who went about doing good, and healing all that were oppressed of the devil; for God was with him. (Acts 10:38).
The anointing that was upon Jesus furnished Him with everything necessary to bring healing and deliverance to all who were oppressed by the devil.

The Spirit of the Lord is upon me, because He hath anointed me to preach the gospel to the poor; He hath sent me to heal the brokenhearted, to preach deliverance to the captives, and recovering of sight to the blind, to set at liberty them that are bruised. (Luke 4:18).

As a believer filled with the Spirit of God, we have received the anointing. God wants us to know how to live in that anointing everyday.
But ye have an unction from the Holy One, and ye know all things. (1 John 2:20).

But the anointing, **which ye have received of Him,** *abideth in you. (1 John 2:27)*

Now He which stablisheth us with you in Christ, and <u>hath</u> anointed us, is God. (2 Corinthians 1:21)

Everything depends on the anointing.
As I write this book, it is my prayer that it will be a blessing to your life and lead you into the anointed life that belongs to you as sons and daughters of God.
I believe the Holy Spirit is challenging you and calling you to come up higher, to reach for the full measure of the In-Christ Life. *Therefore, if any man be <u>in Christ</u> he is a new creature old things are passed away and behold all things are become new (2 Corinthians 5:17).*

Christ means: "Anointed One." If any man be <u>in Christ</u>, or in the anointed one, his life, her life is new.

There are two sides to the Christian life.
There's the **legal side** and the **vital side**.
Or we could say, the <u>legal side</u> and the <u>living side</u>.

The legal side is what the Word of God says belongs to us.
It is the legal document of our inheritance in Christ.

In other words, every promise of God is legally yours. As a child of God, it has been willed to you:
Prosperity, healing, joy, peace, strength, favor.

These are all promises of God to you. It is all yours through Christ.
For all the promises of God <u>in Him</u> are yea, and in him Amen, unto the glory of God by us. (2 Corinthians 1:20).
That is the legal side. They belong to you by inheritance, we are children of God.

The vital side (or living side) is "the experience" of what is legally yours, on the basis of the will; the Word of God;
For example, <u>experiencing</u> the reality of healing manifested in your bodies, joy manifesting in your lives, peace and prosperity actually manifested in your circumstances.

According to the following scripture we get the definition of the anointing as the power to remove burdens and destroy yokes.
And it shall come to pass in that day, that his burden shall be taken away from off thy shoulder, and his yoke from off thy neck, and the yoke shall be destroyed because of the anointing. (Isaiah 10:27)

Then in Luke, we find that the Spirit of the Lord is the anointing that destroys the yokes and removes the burden.

The Spirit of the Lord is upon me, because He hath anointed me to preach the gospel to the poor; He hath sent me to heal the brokenhearted, to preach deliverance to the captives, and recovering of sight to the blind, to set at liberty them that are bruised. (Luke 4:18).

We are so thankful for all the talent in the body of Christ. We are also thankful for those who have taken the time and effort to become educated in theology, the study of God, and to learn Bible truths.

But all the theology in the world cannot compare to a thimble full of the anointing. We appreciate talent, but all the talent in the world on one stage at one time cannot heal one sick body, or lift one heavy burden, or destroy one satanic yoke of bondage.

By all means develop your talents. By all means make the effort to train and develop your mind.
But above and beyond everything else, seek for the anointing, press in for the anointing, ask for the anointing, contend for the anointing and do not be contented or satisfied with anything less than a fresh anointing of the Holy Ghost.

Everything that concerns the kingdom of God must carry the anointing upon it.
It is that anointing that introduces the power of God into every situation.
If you are a singer, you must sing under the anointing.
If you are a teacher, you must teach under the anointing.
If you are a preacher, you must preach under the anointing.

If you are an intercessor, you must pray under the anointing.
If you are a musician, you must play under the anointing.

It is the anointing that moves you from simply doing something to Kingdom ministry.

When you operate under the anointing, you are operating with the supernatural power of God.
In the Old Testament, all of the temple furniture and vessels used in temple service were anointed with oil.

And Moses took the anointing oil, and anointed the tabernacle and all that was therein, and sanctified them.   (Leviticus 8:10)
And the priests were anointed as well.
And Moses took of the anointing oil, and of the blood which was upon the altar, and sprinkled it upon Aaron, and upon his garments, and upon his sons, and upon his sons' garments with him; and sanctified Aaron, and his garments, and his sons, and his sons' garments with him.   (Leviticus 8:30)
The anointing oil sanctified them unto God for His service.
In actual fact, the anointing sanctified in two ways.
1. It sanctified them or separated them from unholy things.
2. It sanctified them or separated them unto God.

So the anointing separates us from the unholy, the impure and even the plain, simple natural or earthly things; *and* **separates us unto God for a heavenly or divine service.**

The following scripture shows us how serious God is about the anointing on our lives.
And ye shall not go out from the door of the tabernacle of the congregation, lest ye die: for the anointing oil of the LORD is upon you. And they did according to the word of Moses. (Leviticus 10:7).

The anointing of the Holy Spirit is a treasure that must be guarded and protected. The oil of the Holy Spirit in our lives must be kept pure and uncontaminated. We must not allow the anointing to be contaminated by the lust desires and appetites of the flesh or it will bring death.

It doesn't necessarily mean that we will die physically but it does certainly mean that our spirit man will experience death. The best Biblical definition of death is not the ending of physical life, but separation from God.

The anointing of the Holy Spirit in our lives must be replenished.
We must have a fresh touch of God upon our lives to be effective in His service.

David, knowing the importance of replenishing the anointing, said:
I shall be anointed with fresh oil. (Psalm 92:10).

In the natural, when oil gets old it stinks. Also, as oil is used it begins to wear thin and lose its viscosity. That word means <u>its ability to reduce friction.</u>

Nothing is worse than a Christian who is trying to operate on an old anointing, trying to operate on a relationship they once had with God but do not have anymore.

Fresh oil has a beautiful aroma, <u>but when it gets old it stinks.</u>
Fresh oil makes things run smoothly. It takes the squeaks out, and it gets rid of the friction.

When the oil of the anointing gets old in a believer's life, they begin to give off an offensive odor in the spirit realm. They are no longer attractive. They begin to become squeaky and irritable.

Not only are they no longer effective for the kingdom of God, they actually begin to discourage others from the kingdom of God.
We must continually examine ourselves to be sure that we are walking and living with a fresh anointing upon our lives.

We must also guard ourselves against the waste of the anointing.
If the devil cannot get you to give up the anointing, and he cannot take the anointing from you, then he will go to every extreme to try to get you to waste the anointing.

Something is considered wasted when it is used beyond what is necessary.
If it takes one shot of Raid to kill an ant and you use half the can that is considered a waste.

Waste also means, to use for a different or lesser purpose or thing than it was created or intended for; to use on something or for something that is below its worth and value.

For example: It would be a waste to spray an ant with an eighty-dollar bottle of perfume.
It would probably kill the ant, but you can buy a whole can of Raid for four dollars and kill thousands of ants.

I want us to examine this concept of wasting the anointing.
Let's look at a man who had a definite and strong anointing on his life. His name was Samson.

The Bible says: *And there was a certain man of Zorah, of the family of the Danites, whose name was Manoah; and his wife was barren, and bare not.*

And the angel of the LORD appeared unto the woman, and said unto her, Behold now, thou art barren, and bearest not: but thou shalt conceive, and bear a son. Now therefore beware, I pray thee, and drink not wine or strong drink, and eat not any unclean thing:

For, lo, thou shalt conceive, and bear a son; and no razor shall come on his head: for the child shall be a Nazarite unto God from the womb: and he shall begin to deliver Israel out of the hand of the Philistines. (Judges 13:2-5).

When we look at Samson's life we see a man who was anointed by God. He was a man who had a divine call and destiny upon his life. His birth was supernatural, he was born to a barren woman, and he was a Nazarite from the day of his birth, which means, one who has a covenant with God.

Very early in his life he felt the touch of God upon his life.
And the woman bare a son, and called his name Samson: and the child grew, and the LORD blessed him.

And the Spirit of the LORD began to move him at times in the camp of Dan between Zorah and Eshtaol. (Judges 13:24-25).

Samson was anointed by God

Without a doubt, no question about it, Samson had a special disposition of supernatural strength given to him by God.

But how much of that supernatural endowment was used for the purpose it was given, and how much of it was wasted?

As I study Samson's life, I find that his life was one long soap opera. He was a drama king.

You know how soap operas are?
You could miss a year, then turn on the TV one day and it's just like you never missed a show because it's just one long repetitive drama.

A lot of people are like that, you haven't seen them for two years, but the next time you see them, they're still stuck in the same rut, fighting the same battles, going around the same mulberry bush.
They're still talking about divorce, still can't pay their bills, still can't get along with anyone in the church, still talking about all their aches and pains, still talking about how everyone is against them, and no one cares and no one understands.

Samson's life was one long drama. It had all the ingredients of a modern day, best selling soap opera.
There was deception, betrayal, bitterness, vengeance, infidelity, lust, greed, sex, and murder.

As a matter of fact, the sad truth is Samson never did anything from a right motive. He didn't do anything from the perspective of bringing glory to God or helping his brothers. Every act of Samson's life was self-motivated, self-serving, and self-pleasing.
If any good came out of Samson's actions, it was purely co-incidental. In other words, it didn't happen because of a well thought-out plan, or an intention to please God.

The truth is: Samson did the Lord's work more by accident than he did by design.
Yes, he killed a lion with his bare hands. But it was a

confrontation that happened because he was running around in Philistine territory, where he should not have been, looking at what he should not have been looking at.

This is what I call wasting the anointing. Yes, Samson was anointed, but Samson's actions were always a fleshly response to a situation that he created.
For example: He goes and kills thirty Philistines. Then he takes their garments to give to men who found out his riddle from his wife.
He played the game and he lost. He played with fire and got burned.

And Samson said unto them, I will now put forth a riddle unto you: if ye can certainly declare it me within the seven days of the feast, and find it out, then I will give you thirty sheets and thirty change of garments:

But if ye cannot declare it me, then shall ye give me thirty sheets and thirty changes of garments. And they said unto him, put forth thy riddle, that we may hear it.

And he said unto them, Out of the eater came forth meat, and out of the strong came forth sweetness. And they could not in three days expound the riddle.

And it came to pass on the seventh day, that they said unto Samson's wife, Entice thy husband, that he may declare unto us the riddle, lest we burn thee and thy father's house with fire: have ye called us to take that we have? is it not so?

And Samson's wife wept before him, and said, Thou dost but hate me, and lovest me not: thou hast put forth a riddle unto the children of my people, and hast not told it me. And he said unto her, Behold, I have not told it my father nor my mother, and shall I tell it thee?

And she wept before him the seven days, while their feast lasted: and it came to pass on the seventh day, that he told her,

because she lay sore upon him: and she told the riddle to the children of her people.
 And the men of the city said unto him on the seventh day before the sun went down, what is sweeter than honey? And what is stronger than a lion? And he said unto them, if ye had not plowed with my heifer, ye had not found out my riddle.
 And the Spirit of the LORD came upon him, and he went down to Ashkelon, and slew thirty men of them, and took their spoil, and gave change of garments unto them which expounded the riddle. And his anger was kindled, and he went up to his father's house. (Judges 14:15-19).

So now Samson is angry with his Philistine wife and runs away.

After awhile Samson cools off and comes back and wants to be intimate with his wife, <u>but her father gave her to the one who was the best man at their wedding.</u>

But it came to pass within a while after, in the time of wheat harvest, that Samson visited his wife with a kid; and he said, I will go in to my wife into the chamber. But her father would not suffer him to go in. (Judges 15:1).
 But Samson's wife was given to his companion, whom he had used as his friend. (Judges 14:20).

 And her father said, I verily thought that thou hadst utterly hated her; therefore I gave her to thy companion: is not her younger sister fairer than she? Take her; I pray thee, instead of her. (Judges 15:2).

Now Samson is angry again, so he goes and catches three hundred foxes and ties them together in pairs, and puts a fire brand between the tails of each pair. Then he turns them loose into the Philistine corn fields.

And when he had set the brands on fire, he let them go into the standing corn of the Philistines, and burnt up both the shocks, and also the standing corn, with the vineyards and olives. (Judges 15:5).

Samson's only motivation is vengeance (pay back).
And Samson said concerning them, now shall I be more blameless than the Philistines, though I do them a displeasure. (Judges 15:3).

Never once does the Bible say, the Lord said unto Samson. Never once did Samson act on the Lord's part because of his love for God.

No, every one of his actions were birthed out of his human emotions, his anger, and his vengeance.
Samson's actions were for Samson.
Samson was acting totally contrary to the principles of God.
Samson theorized that what he did to the Philistines was justified because they had hurt him.
His mind set was, two wrongs *do* make a right.
You hurt me. I hurt you and we're even.

These were battles of his own making. In other words, they were battles he should not have had. They were a waste of his anointing.
Many of God's people today are fighting battles that they should not be fighting.

Why do I say that? because there is no reward.
It is a waste of the anointing to fight battles that have no spoils or reward.

One of the devil's most effective tactics against the believer is to get them into struggles, battles, and confrontations; that are fleshly in nature, and drain their anointing, but produce no real victory.

If the battle you are fighting has no eternal significance (meaning that if it doesn't in some way reveal God to you in a greater way), then it is a waste of your anointing. It is a waste of your time, a waste of your energies.
I am not saying that a real battle will not take your time or energies, or that it will not wear you out and leave you exhausted. What I am saying is that if it is a battle you should be fighting, then you will come out of that battle with a significant victory.

It may be healing in your body. It may be your loved ones salvation. It may be a greater revelation of the power of God and a deeper more intimate relationship with God.

It may be breaking the spirit of debt and lack. It may be stronger faith and confidence in God and His Word.
It may be a new level of anointing and authority in your ministry.
It can be a thousand different things but the bottom line is that you will gain something through the fight that will bring a greater revelation of God and a greater relationship with God.

One of the devil's greatest and most effective tools against the child of God is to draw them into pointless, meaningless, useless battles that induce them to draw unnecessarily on the anointing that is in them and on their lives.

If the devil can induce you to expend your anointing and your resources on fleshly, carnal, earthly conflicts, then you will not have the spiritual resources you need to deal with the battles that matter, and that affect souls for time and eternity.

For we wrestle not against flesh and blood, but against principalities, against powers, against the rulers of the darkness of this world, against spiritual wickedness in high places. (Ephesians 6:12).

The apostle Paul is using this analogy to tell us that the devil will try to draw us into battles that are fleshly in nature. If he accomplishes this, then he has deterred us from the real battlefront. We are no threat to him or his kingdom.

That word "wrestle" is a term that describes an intense up close struggle.
Many times a man will get his opponent in a hold that is like a vice. The opponent will struggle with all his strength just to try and break free of that hold.

But for all the energy and strength that is expended, it seems like very little gain, if any, is made.
This is the devil's plan: to get Christians all wrapped up in fleshly battles, drama that drains their anointing and yet produces no results for the kingdom of God.

Samson was the king of drama; his life was a mess. Yet in the middle of all this drama, he was still anointed. But Samson wasted his anointing on drama.

Every draw upon the anointing in Samson's life was to <u>serve</u> himself, or <u>save</u> himself from a self-created dilemma.

What a contradiction it is, to be so strongly anointed, and yet be so carnal, so fleshly, and so selfish.

Samson's life shows us that the anointing is no substitute for good character. His life shows us that we are responsible to cultivate our own spirits, to hold ourselves accountable for our actions, and to learn from our mistakes.

If you study Samson's life, it would <u>not</u> be to find an example of integrity (he had none), or self-control (he had none), or compassion (he had none), or patience (he had none).

One of the saddest lessons we learn from Samson's life is that it is possible to waste your anointing; to waste your spiritual resources in an arena that has no kingdom impact whatsoever.

Let me say it another way. Just because you win a battle does not necessarily mean you are victorious. It is possible to win and yet lose.

Let me give you an illustration.
And it came to pass, after the year was expired, <u>at the time when kings go forth to battle, that David sent Joab, and his servants with him, and all Israel; and <u>they destroyed the children of Ammon, and besieged Rabbah.</u> But David tarried still at Jerusalem.</u> (2 Samuel 11:1).
The Bible says it was the time of year when kings go out to battle but <u>David stayed home</u>.

In the time when King David should have been on the battlefield leading his army into battle, he was at home. David sent his captain in his place.

On the surface it looks like a great victory was won, but while Joab was out winning a battle, David was losing the war.

While Joab won a great victory, David fell victim to the spirit of lust and committed adultery with Bethsheba. Ultimately, he had her husband, Uriah, killed in battle.

While on one front a small battle was won, on the other front the war was lost. If I win a natural, fleshly battle or conflict, yet waste all my spiritual resources in the fight, I may have won the conflict. But I lost the most important thing, which is the anointing that I need for true spiritual warfare. Even though I may have won the flesh battle, the devil has actually won the war. He has seduced me into wasting my anointing, using my anointing and my spiritual resources for something that is beneath it, and really unworthy of my attention.

I do not question whether you are anointed or not. What I want to know is, how much of the anointing is being wasted and how much is being utilized to bring true spiritual victories and advance the Kingdom of God?

How much of your prayer time and energy is spent just praying yourself out of one pit and one problem after another? How much of your prayer time is wasted on drama, things that have no impact on your destiny or the destiny of others?

It is certainly not wrong to pray for yourself and your own needs, but as a believer you should reach a place in God where you are standing on solid ground, and you are able to reach into the pit and pull someone else out.

Jesus said: The Lord's Spirit, or we could say "the anointing", is upon me because He hath anointed me. Then He proceeds to tell us what He was anointed for, and every single thing He says speaks of service to others.

The Spirit of the Lord is upon me, "because" he hath anointed me to preach the gospel to the poor; he hath sent me to heal the brokenhearted, to preach deliverance to the captives, and recovering of sight to the blind, to set at liberty them that are bruised. (Luke 4:18).

Let's look at another story in the Bible about wasted resources. We will identify this as the anointing, because the anointing is the greatest resource we have.

And He said, A certain man had two sons And the younger of them said to his father, Father, give me the portion of goods that falleth to me. And he divided unto them his living and not many days after, the younger son gathered all together, and took his journey into a far country, and there <u>wasted his substance</u> with riotous living. (Luke 15:11-13).
It was not wrong that this younger son wanted his inheritance or substance and goods. What was wrong was what he did with it.

He <u>wasted</u> it, through riotous living. In other words, he squandered it or spent it on himself.
He used all of his inheritance to satisfy a selfish, carnal, earthly desire and lifestyle. Everything he did had one aim and that was to please self. Please understand, it is the Father's good pleasure to give you your inheritance. It pleases God when His children want to walk in the resources of heaven.

It brings honor to God when we recognize who we are and that we are the anointed sons of God.

But while we are appropriating our inheritance, and while we are enjoying the mighty anointing of the Holy Spirit, let us learn a lesson from Samson and from the prodigal son. And

Let us determine that we are not going to <u>waste</u> the anointing.

The anointing increases as it is released in ministry and service.

There's a story, in 2 Kings 4:1-6, about a little widow woman whose husband had died and left her in debt, she had nothing in her house except a small pot of oil, or we could say (a small measure of the anointing.) The prophet of God instructed her to borrow from her neighbors' empty vessels, not a few.

Then she was to take that pot of oil (the anointing) and to pour it into those empty vessels. As she poured the oil multiplied and increased until every vessel was filled.

As long as she was pouring the oil, it continued to increase and multiply to supply the need. In other words, as she was ministering and serving, there was a continual supply.

As soon as the last vessel was filled, the oil stayed, or the oil stopped multiplying and increasing. It was limited and constrained to the small measure or size of her little pot.

This shows us that the anointing increases and multiplies through service or through use.

It is a waste of the anointing to have what someone needs and to withhold it from them.

What a waste of heaven's resources it is to have the ability to meet needs and relieve the suffering of those around you, but to keep it to yourself.

Peter and John knew they had what the lame man needed and they opened the floodgates and let it flow into his life.

Then Peter said, Silver and gold have I none; but <u>such as I have give I thee</u>: In the name of Jesus Christ of Nazareth rise *up and walk. And he took him by the right hand, and lifted him up: and immediately his feet and anklebones received strength. And he leaping up stood, and walked, and entered with them into the temple, walking, and leaping, and praising God. (Acts 3:6-8)*

As we receive the anointing, we receive the resources of heaven. We become stewards of that anointing and those resources. If we do not use those resources of the anointing to minister and help others, we are guilty of <u>wasting</u> the anointing and stand in danger of losing it altogether.

We could say it like this: Use it or lose it.

For the kingdom of heaven is as a man travelling into a far country, who called his own servants, and delivered unto them his goods. And unto one he gave five talents, to another two, and to another one; to every man according to his several ability; and straightway took his journey. Then he that had received the five talents went and traded with the same, and made them other five talents.
  And likewise he that had received two, he also gained other two. But he that had received one went and digged in the earth, and <u>hid his lord's money</u>.
  After a long time the lord of those servants cometh, and reckoneth with them. (Matthew 25:14-19).

How many talents each servant received is not really the subject matter of these scriptures. The subject is really what they did with the talents.

According to the following verses, each one put their talents into service, except for the one who received only one talent. He buried his.

18 But he that had received one went and <u>digged in the earth, and hid his lord's money.</u>
19 After a long time the lord of those servants cometh, and reckoneth with them. 20 And so he that had received five talents came and brought other five talents, saying, Lord, thou deliveredst unto me five talents: behold, I have gained beside them five talents more.
21 His lord said unto him, Well done, thou good and faithful servant: thou hast been faithful over a few things, I will make thee ruler over many things: enter thou into the joy of thy lord.
22 He also that had received two talents came and said, Lord, thou deliveredst unto me two talents: behold, I have gained two other talents beside them.
23 His lord said unto him, Well done, good and faithful servant; thou hast been faithful over a few things, I will make thee ruler over many things: enter thou into the joy of thy lord.
24 Then he which had received the one talent came and said, Lord, I knew thee that thou art an hard man, reaping where thou hast not sown, and gathering where thou hast not strawed: And I was afraid, and went and hid thy talent in the earth: lo, there thou hast that is thine. His lord answered and said unto him, <u>Thou wicked and slothful servant,</u> thou knewest that I reap where I sowed not, and gather where I have not strawed:

His lord did <u>not</u> commend him for safeguarding his talent or resources. In fact, he rebuked him.

And he said unto them Take therefore the talent from him, and give it unto him which hath ten talents. (Matthew 25:18-28).

These talents represent the resources of God, or the anointing of God. The servant in this story lost his talent because he hid it, buried it, and made it inaccessible to others.

His master called him wicked, slothful and unprofitable. His talent was taken away from him. From this king's perspective this talent was being wasted.

So he gave it to someone who would use it.

Jesus told this story to show us how God feels toward those who hide the anointing, or withhold the resources of God, from brothers and sisters in need and a lost and dying world.
Jesus hates waste.

When the disciples finished feeding the multitude, Jesus said that He did not want anything to be wasted.
When they were filled, He said unto His disciples, gather up the fragments that remain, <u>that nothing be lost</u>. (John 6:12).

Jesus considered it to be wasted if it was not eaten or did not meet needs.
How many of God's people are guilty of wasting the anointing?

If you hide your light you are wasting the anointing.
If Christ in you, is not flowing out of you, ministering to others, then you are wasting the anointing.

Remember one definition of wasting is to use excessively, or to use more than is needed.

How does that apply to the anointing? Well, God has placed within His anointed ones more than enough, a plentiful supply. He even calls those resources, rivers of living waters. To keep those resources locked up inside is a waste of the anointing, just as much as the wicked servant who buried his talent in the earth.

The Holy Spirit is a river, the anointing flows like a river.
May God help us to be a channel through which the anointing flows and not a dam that stands in His way.

If what you receive from God stops with you, then it is a waste. It was not given to you to put on a shelf in the cabinet but to be poured from vessel to vessel.

Jesus said: "Ye are the light of the world."
"Ye are the salt of the earth."
Everyone knows that salt is worthless as long as it stays in the cabinet, and light is worthless if it is hid under a bushel.
Jesus said: the anointing in us, which is the Holy Ghost, would flow out of our innermost being like a river.

The anointing is the yoke-destroying, burden removing power of God that enables us and empowers us to serve others.

There is more to the anointing than shaking, it's about serving.
According to the scriptures, Samson shook.
Samson shook, but <u>Samson never served anyone</u> but himself.

*And she said the Philistines be upon thee Samson. And he awoke out of his sleep, and said; I will go out as at other times and **<u>shake myself</u>**. And he wist not that the Spirit of the Lord had departed from him. (Judges 16:20).*

But let me say while we're on the subject, it's all right to shake.
Someone said: I don't believe all that shaking is necessary. I just don't think we need all that jumping around and shouting

and hollering and stuff. I believe it's all just emotionalism. And some will even say, it's in the flesh.

Well, somebody should have told that to David. The Bible says he danced before the Lord with all <u>his</u> might and it doesn't say one thing about the Spirit coming upon him.

And David danced before the LORD <u>with all his might</u>; and David was girded with a linen ephod.
15 So David and all the house of Israel brought up the ark of the LORD with shouting, and with the sound of the trumpet. 16 And as the ark of the LORD came into the city of David, Michal, Saul's daughter looked through a window, and saw King David <u>leaping</u> and <u>dancing</u> before the LORD; and she despised him in her heart. (2 Samuel 6:14-16).

So there is something about the shaking that says to God, I'm available.
In other words, action on my part produces a reaction on God's part.

When I shake I'm just telling God, I'm available. When I clap my hands, it means my hands are available. When I stomp my feet or dance, it means my feet are available to go wherever you want me to go.

When I lift my voice and shout and praise God, it means my voice is available to proclaim your word.
It's a signal to the anointing that I'm available. It's my way of saying, here I am God, you can use me.

If you see me shaking, I don't want to offend you but I'm just telling God I'm available.

Why don't you pause right now. Tell God, "I am available.
Take my hands and my feet and my voice, and use me."
It's all right to shake, but when you're through shaking it is time to serve.

If our shaking does not translate into serving, it is a waste of the anointing.
When Jesus rebuked Martha, He was not rebuking her for her desire to serve. He was chiding her for the fact that she was neglecting to spend time with Him. She was trying to serve in her own strength and abilities apart from the Lord.

Let's take a minute and look at these scriptures. We will see how Jesus addressed the difference between Mary and Martha.

Now it came to pass, as they went, that He entered into a certain village: and a certain woman named Martha received Him into her house. 39 And she had a sister called Mary, which also sat at Jesus' feet, and heard His word. 40 But Martha was cumbered about much serving, and came to Him, and said, Lord, dost thou not care that my sister hath left me to serve alone? bid her therefore that she help me.
41 And Jesus answered and said unto her, Martha, Martha, thou art careful and troubled about many things:
42 But one thing is needful: and Mary hath chosen that good part, which shall not be taken away from her. (Luke 10:38-42).

It was out of balance for Martha to try to serve others, while neglecting her relationship with the Lord.

But it would have been just as out of balance for Mary to sit at Jesus feet listening to His words and soaking up His presence but never get up and serve others.

The lesson that Jesus was teaching was not that Mary was better than Martha, but that Mary had the right order.

First, time with God. First, time in His presence. Then, we can serve with the anointing.
It is a waste of the anointing if it doesn't culminate in serving others.

Mary represents a heart for God, a love of His presence and His word. Martha represents hands that are yielded to do the Master's service.

We need both. We need a Mary heart and Martha hands.

We love what Mary represents, but if everyone in the church decided, I'm just going to sit at His feet forever and soak up the anointing, nothing would ever get done for God.

Let's look at another danger we must be aware of as children of God.

Taking The Anointing For Granted.

First of all, what does it mean to take something for granted?

It means to underestimate the value of something. Usually, this is because you make the assumption that you will always have it, and can never lose it.

Samson grew up with the touch of God upon his life. At a young age Samson began to experience the Spirit of the Lord coming upon him.
In reality, God was trying to train Samson by the intervals of the presence and the absence of the anointing.

God wanted Samson to recognize that the source of his supernatural strength was the anointing of God's Spirit.

God wanted Samson to recognize his human weaknesses and insufficiencies; and to appreciate, value, and protect the anointing on his life.

But Samson took the anointing for granted. He began to believe that the anointing was his own power and that it was for his own personal use.

Samson began to step out of bounds, associating with the enemy because he was convinced that the anointing would always be there to deliver him.

But before we point fingers at Samson, we need to think back about how many times we went places and did things that we knew were wrong. But, we counted on the anointing to pull us through?

If we're not careful, we can begin to think just like Samson.

Some of us said to ourselves, God loves me, He doesn't want me to go to hell.
He'll forgive me. He always does. Momma and Daddy are praying for me and God is not going to let their prayers go unanswered.

No doubt Samson's father and mother prayed many prayers for Samson. The anointing did pull him out and did deliver him time after time after time.

But ultimately, it is your covenant with God, and <u>not</u> your anointing that determines your destiny.

Your covenant is your relationship with God.

As harsh as it sounds, you can be anointed and go to hell. The anointing is no guarantee against sin.

Many will say to me in that day. Lord, Lord, have we not prophesied in Thy name? And in Thy name have cast out devils? And in Thy name done many wonderful works? And then will I profess unto them, I never knew you: depart from me, ye that work iniquity. (Matthew 7:22-23)

This scripture is talking about people who had known the anointing (the power of God to cast out devils, etc.) but they did not have a covenant relationship with God.

Samson reached the place where he despised his covenant. He told the enemy the secret of his power.

It was his covenant, his Nazerite vow. Samson reached the place where the only thing left of his vow, his covenant, was the seven locks of his head. This, in keeping with his Nazerite vow (his covenant), had never been cut.
Even after betraying the last trace of his covenant, Samson still believed the anointing would deliver him, and be at his beck and call. He took it for granted that the anointing had always been there and always would be.

After revealing his secret vow, his covenant, Delilah sends immediately for someone to come and shave his head.

And it came to pass, when she pressed him daily with her words, and urged him, so that his soul was vexed unto death; That he told her all his heart, and said unto her, "There hath not come a razor upon mine head; for I have been a Nazarite unto God from my mother's womb:" if I be shaven, then my strength will go from me, and I shall become weak, and be like any other man.

And when Delilah saw that he had told her all his heart, she sent and called for the lords of the Philistines, saying, Come up this once, for he hath shewed me all his heart. Then the lords of the Philistines came up unto her, and brought money in their hand.

And she made him sleep upon her knees; and she called for a man, and she caused him to <u>shave off the seven locks of his head; and she began to afflict him, and his strength went from him.</u>

Then Delilah does the same thing she had done many times before. She yells, Samson, the Philistines be upon you.

And she said, The Philistines be upon thee, Samson. And he awoke out of his sleep, and said, I will go out <u>as at other times before</u>, and shake myself. And he wist not that the LORD was departed from him. (Judges 16:16-20)
Samson jumps to his feet and says, I will shake myself as at other times.
Samson basically said: No problem, the anointing will get me out of this mess. I've got superhuman strength.
I can handle it. I'll just do what I've always done before.

Samson was so convinced that the anointing was his own possession and was his to command, that he was not even aware of that fact that it was gone.

That familiar touch that he'd grown up with from a child was gone, that anointing that had become so common place to him, that he had taken for granted so long was gone.

Time after time after time previously, the anointing had come to his rescue; although he had placed himself in compromising situations, ungodly associations, and sinful relationships.

He thought I'll just jump up like every time before and kill everything in my sight. But this time it was different. His covenant was gone and so was his power, his anointing.
But the Philistines took him, and put out his eyes, and brought him down to Gaza, and bound him with fetters of brass; and he did grind in the prison house. (Judges 16:21).

The anointing was gone and he didn't even know it. It was gone and he never even knew when it left. He was shaking the same, but it wasn't the same. He was dancing the same, but it wasn't the same. He was shouting the same, but it wasn't the same.

He was saying the same words, but there was no power in them. He was going through the same motions, but no yokes were being destroyed, no bondages were being broken.

The anointing he had become so comfortable with, and so familiar with, and so used to, was gone.

One of the most important things we can learn from Samson is: to not take the anointing for granted.

The anointing of the Holy Spirit is exactly that. It is the power of the Holy Spirit coming upon and working through an individual.

It is a gift. It comes from God, and it belongs to God.

It is a treasure to be valued and protected.

The apostle Paul said it this way.
But we have this treasure in earthen vessels that the excellency of the power may be of God and not of us. (Judges 16:21).

Thank God, Samson's life ended on a high note, back in the anointing. In the prison house, his hair began to grow again. Which tells us, that even if you've broken your covenant with God, His grace will restore you.
And let me take it a step farther and tell you, no matter how bad you have messed up and blown it, no matter how far you've fallen, God's grace is greater than your sin.

Don't let the devil condemn you over past failures and past mistakes. Let me also say, don't let religious Pharisees tell you that because you messed up God won't use you, or that you can only do little things from now on.

One of the devil's favorite lines is to tell you, that because you messed up and blew it, God can only use you in little things; that you can only play on the "B Team."
But God wants you to know that no matter how far you have fallen, He is able to pick you up, and lift you to a higher place than you have ever been.

If Samson's life teaches us anything, it is that the grace of God is greater than our sin.

Howbeit the hair of his head began to grow again after he was shaven. Then the lords of the Philistines gathered them together for to offer a great sacrifice unto Dagon their god, and to rejoice: for *they said, Our god hath delivered Samson our enemy into our hand. And when the people saw him, they praised their god: for they said, our god hath delivered into our hands our enemy, and the destroyer of our country, which slew many of us. And it came to pass, when their hearts were merry, that they said, Call for Samson, that he may make us sport. And they called for Samson out of the prison house; and he made them sport: and they set him between the pillars.*

And Samson said unto the lad that held him by the hand, Suffer me that I may feel the pillars whereupon the house standeth, that I may lean upon them. Now the house was full of men and women; and all the lords of the Philistines were there; and there were upon the roof about three thousand men and women that beheld while Samson made sport.
(Judges 16:22-27).

Finally, Samson recognizes that the source of his strength is the Power of God.

And Samson called unto the LORD, and said,
<u>*O Lord GOD, remember me, I pray thee, and strengthen me, I pray thee, only this once, O God,*</u> *that I may be at once avenged of the Philistines for my two eyes.*
And Samson took hold of the two middle pillars upon which the house stood, and on which it was borne up, of the one with his right hand, and of the other with his left.
And Samson said, Let me die with the Philistines. And he bowed himself with all his might; and the house fell upon the lords, and upon all the people that were therein. So the dead which he slew at his death were more than they which he slew in his life. (Judges 16:28-30).

Samson slew more of the enemy at the time of his death than in his whole life. This tells me, the best is yet to come.

You may have taken the anointing for granted, and got your

life all messed up. But if you will repent and renew your covenant with God, He will restore His anointing to your life, and He will use you in a greater way than ever before.

This account says to me: Your best days are ahead.

Samson killed more Philistines at the end than in all his lifetime up to that point.
When he recognized the power was God's and <u>he sought God for his anointing</u>, Samson accomplished more in one minute than in all his life up till that time.
God's will, His plan, His purpose, and His corporate destiny for every child of God is to live in the anointing.

It is the plan and will of God that every believer receives the gift of the Holy Ghost and lives in the power of the anointing.

But ye shall receive power, after that the Holy Ghost is come upon you: and ye shall be witnesses unto me both in Jerusalem, and in all Judaea, and in Samaria, and unto the uttermost part of the earth. (Acts 1:8).

For the promise is unto you and to your children and to all that are afar off even as many as the Lord our God shall call. (Acts 2:39).

If there is anything that the children of God need in this, more than anything else, it is a fresh anointing of the Holy Ghost and power.

I've already said it, but let me say it again: Everything depends on the anointing.

Then he answered and spake unto me, saying, This is the Word of the LORD unto Zerubbabel, saying, "Not by might, nor by power, but by My Spirit, saith the LORD of hosts." (Zechariah 4:6).

Maybe you have been like Samson and taken the anointing for granted, or maybe you have been like the prodigal son and wasted your anointing on carnal selfish pursuits. Maybe you have been like the ungrateful servant who hid his talent in the earth and made it inaccessible to everyone else.

Maybe you have been like Samson and you have wasted your anointing on drama, you have allowed the devil to draw you into fleshly conflicts that have no kingdom impact.

Or maybe you're just tired, because you have been in warfare. You have been doing everything right, but you feel empty and dry.
That's not sin. It just means it is time for a fresh anointing. You need a fresh supply.

Whatever your situation is, God wants to send a fresh anointing on your life right now.
Just look to heaven with me and pray this prayer:
Heavenly Father, I need fresh oil today. It's not by might or power but it is by your anointing. I ask you today to send a fresh anointing upon my life.
Replenish me Lord; I can't make it on old oil. I want my life to be a sweet smelling fragrance.
Holy Spirit, thank you for fresh oil on my life today.
Help me to live <u>in your anointing</u> everyday.
Help me not to waste this precious anointing, and help me not to take it for granted. In Jesus' name I pray Amen.

Chapter 5

Where There Is No Altar The Church Will Falter

Not only will the altar-less church be weak and spiritually impotent, but an altar-less church will also be a Fireless church. Ultimately, the church without an altar will falter.

In I Kings 18:17, Ahab, the king of Israel, meets Elijah with these words: ***Art thou he that troubleth Israel?***

The word "trouble" means to stir up, disturb, to agitate, to afflict with pain or discomfort, to cause mental agitation or distress.
This shows you how far Israel had fallen from God's divine presence and calling.
This king was supposed to lift the standard and was to lead Israel into their divine destiny, and relationship with God. Yet, he was so backslidden that the very presence of Elijah, with his commitment and his consecration and his love for God, disturbed, agitated, even caused Ahab such distress that he called Elijah, "the trouble maker in Israel."

You might as well know this: When you get serious about serving God, when you consecrate yourself to live a holy, separated, sanctified life, you will be viewed by many, and especially by many religious people, as a troublemaker. Why? Because so many Christians are satisfied just to live around the altar, by that I mean, satisfied to be religious; look the part and sound the part, without really selling out to God.

But when you have chosen to live on the altar, which means you have made your life a living sacrifice to God, you will upset this world's system. You will disturb religious people.

I beseech you therefore, brethren, by the mercies of God, that ye present your bodies a living sacrifice, holy, acceptable unto God, which is your reasonable service. (Romans 12:1)

Elijah called the nation of Israel back to the altar.
Elijah is not known through the scriptures as a great preacher. But when the Bible shines the spotlight on Elijah, we see him on the ground with his head between his knees, praying. Elijah showed us what it looks like to have an altar in your life.

The great need of this hour is for men and women who will rebuild the altar, as Elijah did on Mt Carmel.

And Elijah said unto all the people, Come near unto me. And all the people came near unto him. And "he repaired the altar of the LORD that was broken down."(1 Kings 18:30)

When I talk about the altar, I'm not talking about the wooden piece of furniture that we see in the front of far too few churches today. As far as that piece of furniture is concerned, it doesn't matter if its maple, pine, walnut, oak, or two by fours covered with plywood.

It doesn't matter if its 6 feet long, or 12 feet long, or divided into two 6 foot sections, when it's all said and done, that altar, as far as its physical properties are concerned, is just a piece of furniture.
It can't save anybody.
It can't heal anybody.
It can't deliver any body.

It can't pick you up when you fall down.
It can't carry you when you're too weak to walk.
It can't mend a broken heart.
It can't restore a shipwrecked marriage.
It can't break the power of drugs over your life or drive cancer out of your body.

It's just a wooden piece of furniture, separated and set apart for sacred purposes, yes; but still just a piece of furniture.

No, the altar I'm talking about is the altar in the heart.
The altar of a heart that is humbled before God, surrendered to God, consecrated to God, faithful and obedient to God.
The altar I'm speaking of is a life laid down in sacrifice to fulfill the will of God.
Where there is no altar the church will falter.

The dictionary defines the word "falter" as:
1. Move hesitatingly as if about to give way.
2. Be unsure or weak.
3. Walk unsteadily.
4. Stumble.
5. Lose faith, abandon the cause.

This is the message of the hour.
The church is faltering because they have forsaken the altar.

For my people have committed two evils; they have forsaken me the fountain of living waters and they have hewn them out cisterns, broken cisterns, that can hold no water.
(Jeremiah 2:13).

What good is it to have a new house, a new car, a great retirement, and money in five different banks and yet be cold in your soul? The greatest need of the hour is not natural physical prosperity. *"It is soul prosperity."*

For what doth it profit a man if he shall gain the whole world, and lose his soul? (Mark 8:36).

I believe God wants to prosper us in every way, including financially.

The danger is when we substitute natural prosperity for soul prosperity.

Beloved I wish above all things that thou mayest prosper and be in health, even as thy soul prospereth. (III John, verse 2)

But the determining factor is *"as thy soul prospers"*.

The Bible says: *the children of Israel lusted exceedingly in the wilderness and tempted God in the desert.*
Then it says: *God gave them their request but sent leanness to their souls. (Psalm 106: 14-15).*
    Leanness means: thin, emaciated, weak, and sickly.
That means they were physically, naturally satisfied (fat and happy) but their souls were starving to death.

This is happening today in our modern American churches.
We are getting fatter and fatter and more and more filled with natural, carnal, physical things.
We are being entertained, we are being tickled behind the ears, but the soul, the spirit man, is starving to death.
Many of our churches today do not even have altars anymore. The ones that do are mostly covered with dust because they're hardly ever used. They're just for looks.

Again, I know that the altar is just an article of furniture made up of a few pieces of wood, but it is the place where we meet God.

The altar is the meeting place with God. It's where you climb Mt. Moriah and give your Isaacs up to God. It is a place of sacrifice of death to the self-life.

It is a place where we wrestle with God for a changed life. It's the place where Jacob the deceiver, the liar, the usurper and the supplanter dies; and Israel the prince with power is born.

It's the place where:
The sinner finds a savior.
The broken find a healer.
The bound find a deliverer.
The burdened find relief.
The prisoner finds pardon.
The weary find rest.
And the saints find power.

Why is there such a low state of spiritual power in the church today? Why is there so little fire from heaven?

Because the church has forsaken the altar.

Your church may have great programs, great singing, great teaching, great talent, great preaching and great worship. But if you as an individual, and your church, do not have an altar it will falter.

It will be unsteady, it will be unsure and weak, it will stumble, and ultimately it will falter and you will falter, you will lose faith and abandon the cause.

God said: My house shall be called of all nations, a house of prayer.
And he taught, saying unto them, Is it not written, My house shall be called of all nations the house of prayer.
(Mark 11:17).

His house is not a house of dramas and plays, not a house of great preaching, not a house of great fellowship and dinners, not a house of great singers and musicians, but **a house of prayer.**

We know the physical health of a person by their temperature. We know the spiritual health of a person or a church by their spiritual temperature, and you know the spiritual temperature by their commitment to prayer.

No prayer - no power.
Little prayer - little power.
Much prayer - much power.

When I was growing up, one of the greatest ministries in the church was the altar workers.

These were people who had an altar in their own lives and they knew what God could do in hearts and lives at the altar.

They would come alongside of you and labor with you in prayer until you broke through, to salvation or healing or deliverance or the baptism of the Holy Ghost.

My prayer is: God give us altar workers again, not just catchers; not just someone who will cover us up when we fall down.

We need men and women who are not ashamed of tears! They are not worried about their clothes getting wrinkled or their makeup running or their hair getting messed up.

We don't find many altar workers in the church today because now days everybody wants a position.
They want a nametag, they want compensation, and they want their own parking space.

We live in a very selfish time in the church today. It's all about me and my blessing, and every man for himself.
But Jesus didn't come to be served; He came to serve and to give His life a ransom for many.

Elijah took 12 stones representing the 12 tribes of Israel, and he rebuilt the altar. He knew that if he could bring Israel back to the altar, and the altar back to Israel, that he would bring Israel back to God.

I want you to know that the only hope for America today is to come back to the altar. There's no president, no politician, no legislation that can turn this country around.

The only hope for change in America is God -
God back in the home, God back in the schoolhouse, God back in the White House, God back in the church house.

In as much as we can get America back to the altar, we can get America back to God.
Return unto me, and I will return unto you, saith the Lord of hosts. (Malachi 3:7).
I've said it before, but I'll say it again. The greatest structure that we can build in America is not the World Trade Center, in New York.

It is the structure called the altar.
It is in every city, and in every church, and in every home.

It wasn't torn down by terrorists attack, there is no terrorist that could destroy the altar. It was torn down through neglect, and decay, and rejection; in favor of a more comfortable, less painful and humiliating way.

- Only humble people can pray.
- Only weak people can pray.
- Only poor people can pray.
- Only helpless people can pray.
- Only needy people can pray.
- Only people who will admit they need help can pray.

I mean really pray: The kind of prayer that puts hell on high alert, the kind of prayer that can summon the resources of heaven.

The greatest sin of America is not homosexuality. The greatest sin of America is pride.

It's not national pride that we need in America today. It is national humility and total dependence upon God.

If my people, which are called by my name, shall humble themselves, and pray, and seek my face, and turn from their wicked ways; then will I hear from heaven, and will forgive their sin, and will heal their land. (2 Chronicles 7:14).
I know there are some wicked, evil things happening in the world. There are gross and horrible things being done in the world. The world is a very dark and dangerous place. But God is not speaking to the world in this Bible verse.

Wickedness and evil and darkness belong to the world; a sinner sins by nature.

But God is speaking to the church, His people, those who identify themselves with Him, those who go by His name.

God says: if my people will humble themselves and pray, if my people will repent, if my people will turn from their wicked ways.
Then God says: I will hear from heaven and forgive their sin and heal their land.

Revival comes because we rend our hearts and not just our garments. Revival comes because we break up the fallow ground and seek God until He comes and rains righteousness down on us.

Elijah rebuilt the altar:
And if thou wilt make me an altar of stone, thou shalt not build it of hewn stone: for if thou lift up thy tool upon it, thou hast polluted it. (Exodus 20:25).

The stones were whole stones, no tool lifted upon them, for that would pollute the altar before God.

This speaks of:
1. Self-effort, the activity of the flesh.
No flesh, no talent, no skill, no ability is ever a substitute for the anointing.
Upon man's flesh shall it (speaking of the anointing) not be poured, neither shall ye make any other like it, after the composition of it: it is holy, and it shall be holy unto you. (Exodus 30:32).

2. God doesn't want fragments of our lives.

Then Elijah said:
I will dress the other bullock, "I will present it as God has required."
Contrary to popular opinion, God will not accept any old offering or sacrifice.

That ye present your bodies, a living sacrifice holy and acceptable to God. (Romans 12:1).

You make the table (altar) of the lord contemptible. How? Ye offer the blind, the lame, and the sick to me. (Malachi 1:7-8).

In other words: There is an acceptable pleasing sacrifice to the Lord, and there is an unacceptable offering to the Lord.

Finally, Elijah called for an investment of the people. He asked for 12 barrels of water when there hadn't been a drop of water from the sky or dew upon the ground for three and a half years.

If you don't ever make an investment in anything, you don't really care about it.
Pursuit is the proof of desire.

If you really want something, you will spend time in the pursuit of it.
You know the importance of a thing by the time you are willing to give to it.

How much time do you give to really seeking God?
How much time do you spend on your face compared to how much time you spend on face-book?

We live in a technological, information age. We are connected to everything and everyone, except the one who matters most - God.

So many people today feel like they would die if they lost their phone, or had to go without their phone for a day.
But many of those same people can go days and even weeks without talking to God.

The 12 barrels of water, in time of drought and famine, was a tremendous sacrifice.
(Not to mention, the hard work required to get it to the altar.)

The point is this: **If we really want to experience a move of God, it is going to cost us something.**

There will never be fire from heaven without an investment of water.
Water, in the time of famine; <u>12 barrels of water, during a drought, was a great sacrifice.</u>

It seems today that the church is in a spiritual drought, the drought of dry eyes.

We don't see many tears on the altar anymore.
But it is still true; the fire will fall when the wood is wet.

There must be more time around the altar.
Elijah had them <u>dig a trench around the altar.</u>
If we are going to see the power of God manifested, there has to be <u>more work around the altar.</u>

If we don't have any time to pray, then we should not think it strange that we are powerless, and that there is no supernatural fire in our midst.

Prayer is hard work; hard on the flesh, hard on pride, hard on the carnal mind.

Notice the scripture says: and he made a trench about the altar. This shows us how vitally connected the preaching of the Word is with prayer.

If we would see preaching that results in changed lives, we must saturate the Word with prayer.

But we will give ourselves continually to <u>prayer, and to the ministry of the Word.</u> (Acts 6:4).

Then as the water covered the altar and sacrifice, <u>*it filled the trench round about.*</u>

This is speaking of a deep work of the Spirit, more than a touch; transformation which comes through the **soaking saturation of the Word of God.**

You can't just hear the word preached or even taught.

You have got to let it <u>soak</u> into your life; you have to let it break up the fallow ground.
After Elijah had done all he could do from the earth side, He calls on God; not just any God but the God who answers by fire.

And Heaven bent low to hear the voice of the old prophet, and God, Himself answered him, and suddenly…

The fire from heaven fell and consumed the sacrifice, the altar, the stones of the altar, and licked up the water in the trench, and licked up the dust.

The supernatural fire of God always falls on the divine order of God.

If we desire the divine supernatural fire of God in our lives, we have to get back to the altar. <u>We have to get our lives in order.</u>

The fire of God falls on a praying church.

My prayer for you, the local church and the American church and every Bible believing child of God, is -
>Lord Send The Fire.

I want to tell you, the most beautiful sound I have ever heard in a church is not the sound of great preachers preaching, and is not the sound of great singers singing.

It is the sound of the church in prayer.
There is something beautiful about the church on her knees.

In its weakness, the church is clothed in majesty and strength and power.

When the church does as Elijah did upon that mountain; and bows its head down between its knees and begins to pray and travail, something powerful happens in the spirit realm.

Hell goes on high alert, demons go to shaking, chains start breaking, yokes are destroyed, captives are delivered and set free, and sons and daughters are birthed into the kingdom of God.

Everything that Satan has ever done to the church or against the church has one prime objective, get them off their knees, keep them off their knees. The devil knows, it's the church on her knees that is going to plunder hell.

The greatest gift that God can give to us as His children is not bigger churches, is not better preachers. It is not more money, or nicer houses, or fancier cars.

The greatest gift that God can give to the church, and you and me personally, is a spirit of prayer.

And I will pour upon the house of David, and upon the inhabitants of Jerusalem, the spirit of grace and of supplications. (Zechariah 12:10).

Where there is no altar, the church will falter.

Somebody said, the fire doesn't fall anymore. But the truth is: Yes, it does; wherever God can find an altar, and a praying people, and lives that are in order according to His Word, and an acceptable sacrifice and wet wood.

Chapter 6

Tarry Until

And, behold, I send the promise of my Father upon you: but tarry ye in the city of Jerusalem, until ye be endued with power from on high. (Luke 24:49).

You and I will never mature spiritually until God's words to us are taken personally as they are written.
It seems that we all have this ability to take God's Word and sift it mentally until all that is left is what we like; and what is comfortable convenient, easy on our flesh, and what is pleasant to us.

It seems that some where between our ears and our hearts is this sifter that sifts out all the commandments and all the conviction, until all we are left with is suggestions and blessings - the things that we already want to do anyway, and the things that make us feel good.

Please don't close the book; I'm not mad at anybody but the devil.
But we need to tell the truth.
That's why our churches today are full of spiritual midgets, or spiritual dwarfs, that should be and could be men and women of great spiritual stature.
They should have and could have great spiritual power and authority with God; but because they won't eat anything but spiritual Cream of Wheat they are spiritual dwarfs.

They should be and could be mighty warriors and soldiers of the cross, but instead, they are "Gerber babies."

What do I mean by Gerber babies?
I mean cute but no power.

By now they should be spiritual warriors, but instead they are spiritual wimps.

They've been raised on strained bananas and pureed prunes because they wouldn't take the Word as it is.

When we take God's Word as it is, it comes loaded with vitamins and nutrients. It comes in a form that requires you to exercise your muscles and use your teeth.

It comes loaded with protein and power.

Jesus said: *The words that I speak unto you they are spirit and life. (John 6:63)*

He meant if you will take them and chew them up and digest them, they will grow you up.

They will build His life into you. They will build His character, His anointing, and His power into you.

Our job as pastors, teachers, and spiritual leaders is **not** to see to it that your diet is always Cream of Wheat and pureed peas and carrots, we also need to set the table with some filet mignon, some prime rib, some pork chops, and some T-bone steaks along with healthy greens, like spinach and broccoli.

You should not be able to digest everything you hear in the same service.

You should leave with your mouth full, still chewing, thinking and meditating on what has been said.
All through the week that Word should be stirring in you, exciting you, inspiring you to pray and to read and study God's Word for yourself.

I hope that this book is more for you than just an in-between meal snack.
I hope that it stirs you up, and makes you think, and births a greater hunger in your life to know God's Word; and experience His presence and His power, personally.

The last command of Jesus to His followers and His disciples before His ascension is found in Acts, Chapter One.

Vs. 4 And, being assembled together with them, commanded them that they should not depart from Jerusalem, but <u>wait for the promise of the Father</u>, which, saith He, ye have heard of me.
Vs. 8 But ye shall receive power, after that the Holy Ghost is come upon you: and ye shall be witnesses unto me both in Jerusalem, and in all Judaea, and in Samaria, and unto the uttermost part of the earth.
(Acts 1:4,8).

Stay in Jerusalem and tarry, wait for the promise!
Tarry there until you be endued with power from on high.

Jesus knew His disciples needed the same power that was in His life. He knew the fire of God would bring the power.
This was not a suggestion. It was a command of the Master.
That commandment has never been withdrawn.

To every disciple, to every follower of the Lord Jesus Christ, the commandment still stands.

Go to Jerusalem and <u>stay there until</u> you be endued with **power from on high**.

Jesus needed that endowment of power and He received it in the river Jordan.

And straightway coming up out of the water, He saw the heavens opened, and <u>the Spirit like a dove descending upon Him</u>. (Mark 1:10).

If the only begotten Son of God needed that Supernatural enduement of power, how much more do we need it?

Go to Jerusalem and wait there till you get the power. Out of at least 500 people Jesus spoke those words to, only 120 made it to the upper room. That means 380 thought they had a better idea and bypassed the upper room.

Beloved, you cannot bypass the upper room and get this power.

There is no alternative route to the power of God. You must go to the upper room and wait until the power comes.

That simply means you must agree with Jesus and never be satisfied until the power of God comes upon you.
To climb up to the upper room means: I agree with Jesus, I will obey His Commandments. I will ask, I will wait, I will knock, I will pray, I will hunger and thirst. I will worship, and I will wait until the power comes.

You shall receive power after the Holy Ghost has come upon you.

We are not just speaking about the gift of tongues, or being baptized in the Holy Ghost.

We don't have to wait for that gift, Jesus has brought that gift within the reach of every blood washed saint.
All you have to do is ask, believe and receive.

No friends, we are not talking about just being baptized in the Spirit and speaking in tongues.

We are speaking about a baptism of power.

After 10 days of waiting in concerted prayer in that upper room, suddenly heaven responded.
Earth cried out and Heaven answered.

Suddenly there came a sound from heaven, as of a rushing mighty wind and it filled all the house where they were sitting. And cloven <u>tongues like as fire set upon each of them</u> and they were all filled with the Holy Ghost and began to speak with other tongues as the Spirit gave them utterance. (Acts 2:2-4)

Fire on their heads produced fire in their mouths.

I am pressed in my spirit today to tell you, that the only church that is going to make a difference in this world, and an eternal impact for the kingdom of God, is the church that has been to the upper room.

They are the churches that have the wind of the spirit pushing them, and tongues of fire upon them, and tongues of fire in their mouths.

Jesus, this is the route to power. You can recalculate all you want, but it will never change.

One hundred and twenty men and women were filled with the Spirit and Power; because they obeyed the Master's command to wait in Jerusalem until the power came.

No one has the authority or power to rewrite the Master's command or the Master's words.

The church today, to a large degree, is powerless because they have bypassed the upper room.

They have chosen alternate routes that are easier on the flesh, that don't require waiting, or praying, or sacrifice or self-denial. And what we are left with is a powerless Church of Gerber babies – cute, but no power.

A form of godliness but denying the power thereof.

One hundred and twenty men and women were filled with the Spirit and Power.

> Do you know why only a hundred and twenty?
> Because only 120 were willing to be emptied;

Emptied of opinions and traditions.
Emptied of self.
Emptied of pride.
Emptied of religion.

Emptied of the world.
Emptied of prejudice.
Emptied of carnal expectations.

And as soon as they were emptied, the Spirit came and filled them. That is why we don't have more Spirit filling today.

People aren't willing to be emptied.

They're full of pleasure, full of self, full of pride, full of tradition, full of religion, full of fear, and full of preconceived ideas.

That's why we have an altar in the church; it is the place where we empty out.
It's been called a mourners bench, not just because sinners mourn their way to repentance, but also because saints mourn when their flesh is being killed.
Saints cry when their flesh is being burned up.

I know the smell of burning human flesh is horrible. But spiritually, God loves the smell of our flesh burning up, It's a sweet incense in His nostrils.

Nothing repulses the Lord more than religious flesh that refuses to die.

The Lord has respect unto the lowly but the proud He knoweth a far-off. (Psalm 138:6).

That means the proud stink and He keeps His distance from them.

You shall receive power after that the Holy Ghost is come upon you.

I feel an urgency in my spirit today to exhort you, nay to warn the church, that we are sailing through perilous waters today. And a church without fire is a church without power, and a church without the baptism of the Holy Ghost is a church without power.

I love you, I want you to like me, but I'm not going to rewrite Jesus' words or dilute them, or puree them until you can't recognize them.

Jesus said the church must have power. The source of this power is the baptism of the Holy Ghost.

Please understand that the war is no longer in a distant land, far away overseas in another country.

No, it is in our country, our state, our community, our schools, and our homes.
It is a spiritual battle. It cannot be won with natural flesh and blood weapons.

It must be fought in the spirit and the only ones who can fight on that level are those who are full of the Holy Ghost and power.

For the weapons of our warfare are not carnal, but mighty <u>through God</u> to the pulling down of strong holds.
(2 Corinthians 10:4).

It is the will of God that every single person who has been plunged beneath Calvary's flow and washed in Jesus blood, also be baptized with the Holy Ghost and fire.

It disturbs me when people act as though the baptism of the Holy Spirit is some side note; some kind of take it or leave it proposition.
I'm going to say this, and I make no apologies for it.

The Holy Ghost Baptism with the accompanying evidence of speaking in other tongues is not an optional accessory, it is necessary equipment.

Be filled with the spirit was <u>the command</u> of the apostle. Notice it was not a suggestion.

And be not drunk with wine, wherein is excess; but <u>be filled</u> with the Spirit...(Ephesians 5:18).

Are you full of the spirit? Or are you full of self and topped off with the spirit?
Are you full? Are you on fire? Does the fire of God burn in your belly?
   The only church that is going to stand in these dark days is the church that walks in the light of God's Word and is filled with His Spirit and Power.

Tarry until you be endued with power from on High.

For the promise is unto you and unto your children and to all them that are afar off even as many as the Lord our God shall call. (Acts 2:39).

Jesus said: *And, behold, I send the promise of my Father upon you: but <u>tarry ye in the city of Jerusalem, until ye be endued with power from on high.</u> (Luke 24:49).*

The promise of this power from Heaven, this Holy Ghost and fire, is to every blood washed child of God.

This is where we start to lose a lot of people. We live in a microwave society, and we want everything yesterday.

We don't want to have to wait for anything.
We drive through the McDonald's drive through and fuss because it takes two minutes to get our order.
We stand in front of the microwave and tap our foot because it takes a full 60 seconds to reheat our burrito.
We are a Microwave Society.

But the truth is, there are some things that don't come instantly.

There are some things that you have to wait for, seek for, ask for, pray for, hunger and thirst for.
And you won't get them until you do.

Even the "suddenly" in Acts, chapter two, came after ten long days of waiting, of tarrying, of hungering and thirsting.

Scripture states, But <u>they that wait upon the LORD</u> shall renew their strength; they shall mount up with wings as eagles; they shall run, and not be weary; and they shall walk, and not faint. (Isaiah 40:31).

For the most part, believers have lost the art of tarrying.

We are a very impatient people.

**But waiting on God is the price of receiving Power.
Power comes upon those who spend time in His presence.**

First, we have to build the altar.
Then, we have to put the wood in order. In the scriptures, wood speaks of humanity, so we have to get our lives in order in obedience to God's Word.
Next, we have to put the sacrifice on the altar.
Then, we dig a trench around the altar, which means the Word of God must penetrate our hearts.
And, we have to soak it all in prayer.

Finally, we have to admit: we cannot set ourselves on fire.

Remember Elijah said: "Put no fire under it."

That means the fire must come from Heaven.

Friend: God still answers by fire wherever He finds an acceptable sacrifice.

If you are willing to build the altar, and you are willing to provide your life a living sacrifice:
God will send the fire.

Dear friend: My prayer for you today is not that God will just touch you and bless you, but that He will send fire from Heaven and consume your life.

For our God is a Consuming Fire.

About The Author

Author, Terry Sisney has been in ministry for over thirty-five years. He has spoken in conferences, camp meetings and revivals, with a teaching and preaching ministry that focuses on the maturing of the saints.

He and his wife, Pam, have been in ministry together for 30 years. They have ministered side by side in full time evangelistic ministry for over fifteen years, as well as pastoral ministry.

Now as an author, teacher and pastor, he serves the body of Christ as Senior Pastor of Grover Beach Pentecostal Church of God, in Grover Beach, California.

To Contact Author
Write

Terry Sisney
1120 Brighton Ave
Grover Beach Ca. 93433

Please include your prayer
Requests when you write.

Other Books By Author

<u>Over Comers Series</u>
You're Supposed To Win
Keep On Walking
The Indispensable Gift (Holy Spirit)
Taking It Back

<u>Other Books By Author</u>
A New Chapter
When You Pray
Armed And Dangerous
Abundant Life Lessons

The author would like to extend a special and personal thanks to the Congregation of Grover Beach Pentecostal Church of God for their love and faithful, prayerful support.

FIRE FROM HEAVEN

Terry Sisney

Printed in Great Britain
by Amazon